CROCODILIANS
Survivors from the Dinosaur Age

by Josep Piqué
Illustrated by Gabriel Casadevall and Ali Garousi

Gareth Stevens Publishing
MILWAUKEE

For a free color catalog describing Gareth Stevens' list of high-quality books and multimedia programs, call 1-800-542-2595 (USA) or 1-800-461-9120 (Canada). Gareth Stevens Publishing's Fax: (414) 225-0377. See our catalog, too, on the World Wide Web: http://gsinc.com

The editor would like to extend special thanks to Richard Sajdak, Aquarium and Reptile Curator, Milwaukee County Zoo, Milwaukee, Wisconsin, for his kind and professional help with the information in this book.

Library of Congress Cataloging-in-Publication Data

Piqué, Josep.
    [Cocodrilo. English]
    Crocodilians: survivors from the dinosaur age / by Josep Piqué; illustrated by Gabriel Casadevall and Ali Garousi.
        p. cm. – (Secrets of the animal world)
    Includes bibliographical references (p. 31) and index.
    Summary: Describes the physical characteristics, behavior, and natural environment of various members of the ancient crocodile family.
    ISBN 0-8368-1496-7 (lib. bdg.)
    1. Crocodiles–Juvenile literature. [1. Crocodiles.] I. Casadevall, Gabriel, ill.
II. Garousi, Ali, ill. III. title. IV. Series.
QL666.C925P5713   1996
597.98–dc20   95-54174

This North American edition first published in 1996 by
Gareth Stevens Publishing
1555 North RiverCenter Drive, Suite 201
Milwaukee, Wisconsin 53212 USA

This U.S. edition © 1996 by Gareth Stevens, Inc. Created with original © 1993 Ediciones Este, S.A., Barcelona, Spain. Additional end matter © 1996 by Gareth Stevens, Inc.

Series editor: Patricia Lantier-Sampon
Editorial assistants: Jamie Daniel, Diane Laska, Rita Reitci

Printed in the United States of America

1 2 3 4 5 6 7 8 9 99 98 97 96

CONTENTS

POWERFUL, ARMOR-PLATED ANIMALS

Tropical crocodilians

Crocodilians are vertebrates that inhabit Earth's tropical regions. They live both in water and on dry land. Most species live in rivers, lakes, estuaries, marshes, and swamps. These areas vary according to water quality, salinity, depth, current speed, and vegetation. However, certain crocodilians, such as American and Chinese alligators, live in temperate regions. South American caimans prefer fresh waters; marine crocodiles live in the salty waters of river mouths in Asian and Pacific tropics.

The crocodile's teeth are weapons for gripping and tearing the prey it catches in its watery environment.

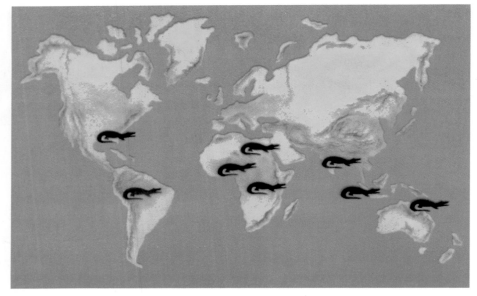

Crocodilian distribution around the world.

Prehistoric creatures

Crocodilians are similar in some ways to birds: they have a long external auditory duct, a muscular gizzard, and separate heart chambers. Crocodilians also build nests with vegetation and look after their young. Crocodiles and birds probably had a common ancestor that lived as long as 300 million years ago — even before the dinosaurs existed. Today's crocodilians have changed very little since

Alligators conserve their ancestors' characteristics, such as the scales covering their skin.

that time, although the spine has become more flexible. Crocodilians are able to eat and breathe at the same time.

The crocodilian family tree.

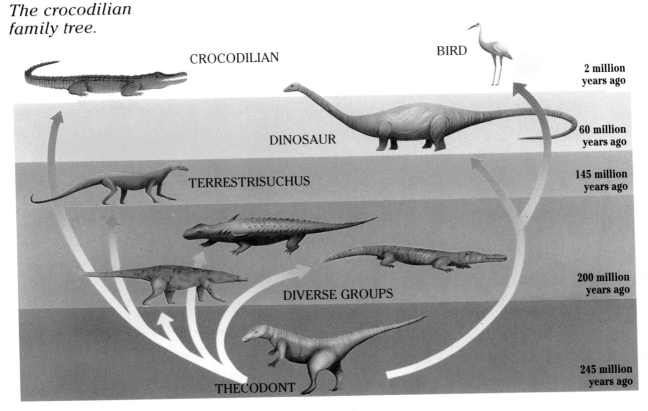

CROCODILIAN

BIRD

DINOSAUR

TERRESTRISUCHUS

DIVERSE GROUPS

THECODONT

2 million years ago

60 million years ago

145 million years ago

200 million years ago

245 million years ago

Crocodilian relatives

Three subfamilies make up the large crocodilian group: crocodiles; alligators and caimans; and gavials. They all have a bony skeleton and a scale-covered body, and they all lay eggs. The crocodile family has fourteen species, all having a cone-shaped snout and a fourth tooth in the lower jaw that shows even with the mouth closed. Crocodilians vary in size and can measure between 5 and 23 feet (1.5 and 7 meters) in length. The seven species of alligators and caimans include Chinese and American alligators, black caimans, spectacled caimans, dwarf caimans, and jacaré caimans. Gavials have a long, thin snout, rounded at the sides with small teeth. Gavials live in the rivers of northern India and measure up to 21 feet (6.5 m) long.

GAVIAL

CHINESE ALLIGATOR

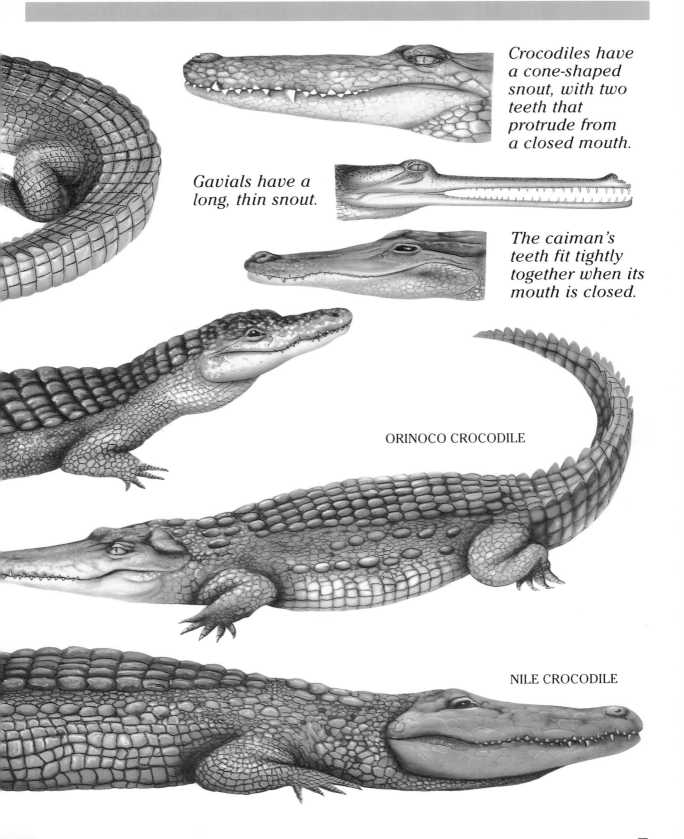

Crocodiles have a cone-shaped snout, with two teeth that protrude from a closed mouth.

Gavials have a long, thin snout.

The caiman's teeth fit tightly together when its mouth is closed.

ORINOCO CROCODILE

NILE CROCODILE

INSIDE THE CROCODILE

The crocodile's body is ideal for swimming fast. It moves its tail back and forth to drive through the water. The crocodile raises its feet up against its body as it swims to reduce friction.

POWERFUL RUDDER
The tail serves as a rudder and propulsion system for moving in the water.

DORSAL ARMOR
Certain species of crocodiles are entirely covered with ossified armor-plating on the inside. Others have fewer scales on their body, which means they have less protection but more mobility.

POWERFUL JAWS
Only the lower jaw, or mandible, can move. The upper jaw stays in place. This mobility allows the crocodile to gobble large prey.

SIGHT
The crocodile's vertical pupils enable it to see in bad light conditions.

SHARP SENSE OF SMELL
Nostrils are on the top end of the snout.

SNOUT

EYE

BRAIN

SKULL

LUNG

NOSTRILS

TEETH
The crocodile uses its teeth to grab prey and drag it under the water to drown it before devouring it.

HEARING
The crocodile's sense of hearing is highly developed. Its ears are covered by a lid of movable skin to keep water out during dives.

HEAD

ESOPHAGUS

TOOTH REPLACEMENT
All the crocodile's teeth are long and cone-shaped, and they can last up to two years. Those at the end of the snout are replaced more often than those nearest the throat.

WALKING, RUNNING, and CRAWLING
Crocodiles usually walk at a steady pace, but, if threatened, they can run as fast as 1.8-10.5 miles (3-17 km) per hour.

TRACHEA

HEART

FRONT FEET

8

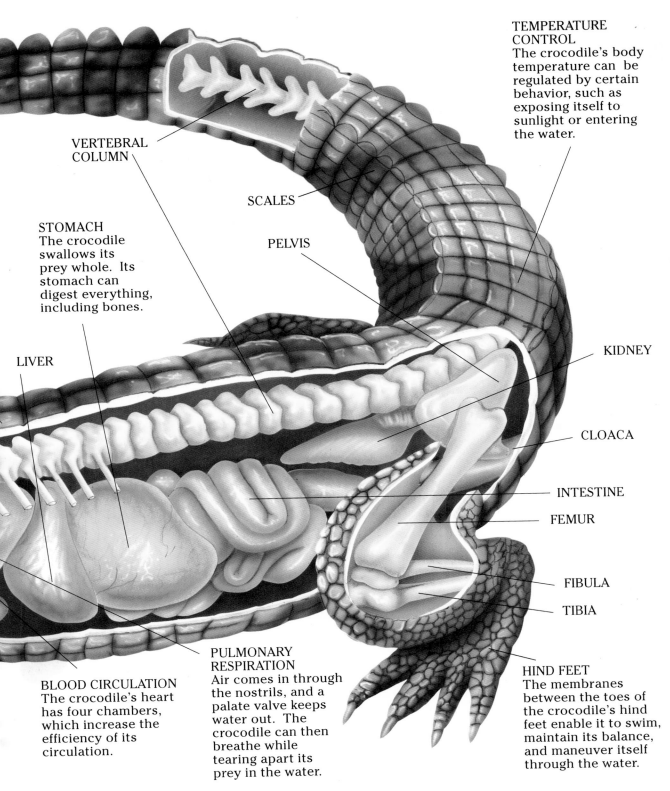

TEMPERATURE CONTROL
The crocodile's body temperature can be regulated by certain behavior, such as exposing itself to sunlight or entering the water.

VERTEBRAL COLUMN

SCALES

PELVIS

STOMACH
The crocodile swallows its prey whole. Its stomach can digest everything, including bones.

LIVER

KIDNEY

CLOACA

INTESTINE

FEMUR

FIBULA

TIBIA

BLOOD CIRCULATION
The crocodile's heart has four chambers, which increase the efficiency of its circulation.

PULMONARY RESPIRATION
Air comes in through the nostrils, and a palate valve keeps water out. The crocodile can then breathe while tearing apart its prey in the water.

HIND FEET
The membranes between the toes of the crocodile's hind feet enable it to swim, maintain its balance, and maneuver itself through the water.

SURVIVORS OF THE PAST

Primitive hunting system

The ancestors of today's crocodilians were small land carnivores with sharp teeth that chased prey by running on their hind legs. Crocodilians today are still predators, and they still have the flat, stout, elongated skull that supports the powerful muscles necessary to crush prey between their jaws. Crocodilians have also kept the bony palate that separates the mouth from the nasal passages and enables the animals to eat or crush their victim while breathing at the same time.

The Central American caiman feeds mainly on fish, frogs, and turtles.

The crocodile has a bony palate that allows the animal to breathe while it eats and also while it is under water.

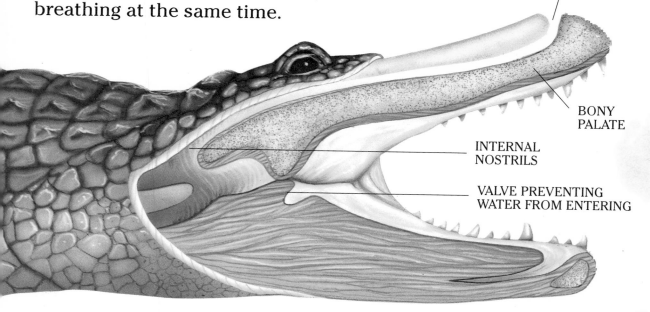

EXTERNAL NOSTRILS

BONY PALATE

INTERNAL NOSTRILS

VALVE PREVENTING WATER FROM ENTERING

that crocodiles can attack people?

Some crocodiles, such as the Nile and marine crocodiles, can attack humans for food. Other species attack mainly because they mistake a human for a prey species. They may also attack in response to a threat, or to defend their territory, their nests, or their young. Such attacks result in wounds that are not commonly fatal. The most usual response of crocodilians to human presence is to hide or become very secretive.

Enemies through time

Different species of carnivorous dinosaurs once captured and ate the adult ancestors of the crocodilians. Today, certain crocodilians are devoured by lions, jaguars, tigers, leopards, and anacondas. But the crocodilians' greatest threat, both then and now, is dying an

The African monitor enjoys a meal of crocodile eggs.

Oviraptor preyed on dinosaur eggs and crocodilian ancestors during Cretaceous times.

early death before reaching adulthood. Crocodilian eggs and young are at greater risk from weather changes and attacks by predators than are adults. Dinosaurs ate the eggs in the past. Today, numerous species of reptiles, birds, and mammals look for opportunities to enjoy them.

Anacondas sometimes attack South American caimans.

Crocodilians and Pangea

Crocodilians first appeared when the world's major landmasses formed a single supercontinent called Pangea. Over time, Pangea separated into several continents, and this caused some animal species to be separated from one another. The animals began to evolve independently, according to their particular habitat. Some crocodilians, for instance, adapted to South America, while others lived in Africa. Still others adapted to life in the sea and moved from one island to another.

The marine crocodile can live in the sea, and this has allowed it to colonize several islands more than 620 miles (1,000 km) from dry land.

Fossils show that crocodilians lived on a single continent called Pangea 200 million years ago.

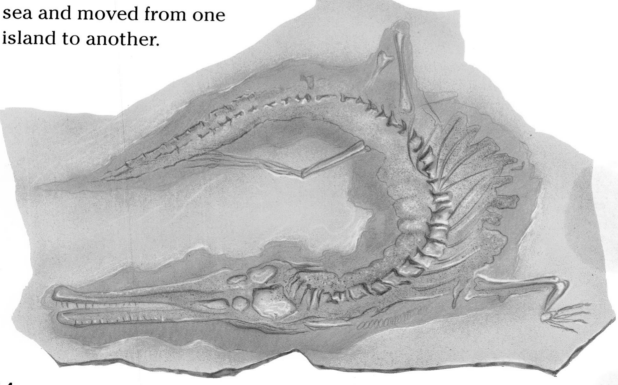

Adaptations

The crocodilian's reptilian eggs helped it move from living in water to life on dry land. The fragile, china-like shell prevents the embryo from losing water during development and also protects it from predators. In earlier times, reptiles prevented water loss through a hard, waterproof layer that covered their scales. Their lungs also provided an efficient respiratory system. Swimming and other body movements helped blood circulation. All these factors allowed the crocodilians to live on land, and they still have these characteristics today.

A reptile's scales prevent dehydration and protect it from enemies.

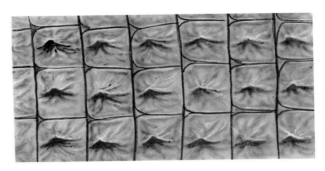

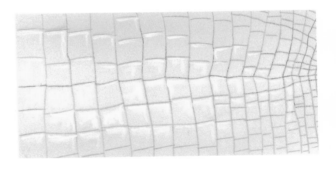

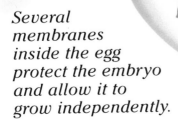

Several membranes inside the egg protect the embryo and allow it to grow independently.

Why didn't crocodilians die with the dinosaurs?

About 65 million years ago, all the dinosaurs and many other animals inhabiting Earth became extinct. Crocodilians, however, survived, and we still do not know why. Some scientists believe Earth's temperature dropped dramatically, but this cannot explain how crocodilians that could not live in cold climates managed to survive. Other scientists believe that the impact of a meteorite wiped out the food source for land and sea animals, and they died. Animals living in fresh water may have been less affected by the climatic changes.

The great extinction eliminated the dinosaurs as well as other animals and plants, but many crocodilians managed to survive.

that the sex of crocodilians depends on the incubation temperature?

For crocodilians, tortoises, and certain lizards, the temperatures at which eggs incubate determine the animal's sex. American alligator males are born if eggs incubate at temperatures between 90° and 93° Fahrenheit (32° and 34° Centigrade). Females are born if temperatures range between 84° and 86°F (29° and 30°C). At incubation temperatures between these two levels, animals of both sexes are born. Depending on the species, the incubation temperatures that determine the sex of the animals can also vary.

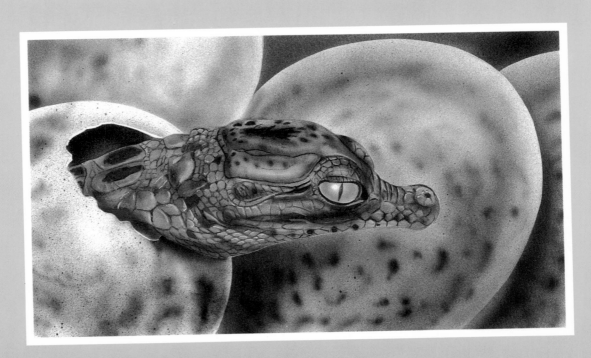

HOW CROCODILIANS LIVE

Territory and mating

The largest and most aggressive crocodiles dominate others and choose their mates, nesting grounds, food, and territory. Crocodiles are most aggressive during the mating season, when they fight rivals. The strongest males defend territory that will provide food, sunlight, and shelter. Large crocodiles attack weak ones by biting the top of the tail behind the hind legs. Adult male crocodiles mate with several females. The animals touch snouts and rub their heads and bodies together,

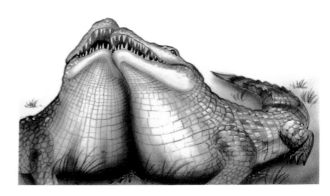

Nile crocodiles rub their bodies together during mating season.

producing bubbles in the mouth and nose. Then they swim around in circles, submerging several times while making certain sounds until they mate.

The American alligator fights to maintain its dominance.

Crocodiles are more tolerant of each other when they live together in a small area.

A pair of Nile crocodiles courting and mating.

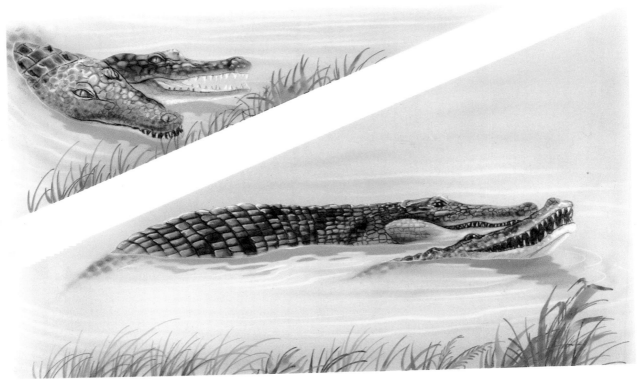

Nests

Four or five months after mating, the African Nile crocodile female digs a nest on the river's bank. When it is about 10 inches (25 cm) deep, she lays up to eighty eggs and covers them with earth. During incubation, which lasts about three months, the female fasts and protects the nest. When the eggs hatch, she digs up the nests, removes the babies, and takes them to the nearest lagoon, where they stay near her for several weeks.

Young caimans are protected and cared for by their mother.

A Nile crocodile digs a nest on the riverbank and lays its eggs.

that some turtles take advantage of the alligator's nest?

The American alligator builds a mounded nest about 3 feet (1 m) high with branches and leaves. Some turtles regularly use the alligator's nest to lay their own eggs. There are several advantages in doing so; for example, the abundance of eggs in one place insures a better survival rate. Also, any predators that attempt to approach the nest do so at the risk of meeting the mother alligator, which is never far away.

PREHISTORIC ANIMALS

Earth's first crocodilians

Crocodilian ancestors were small terrestrial carnivores that could run upright on their hind legs. Gracilisuchus lived in South America about 231 million years ago and measured around 12 inches (30 cm) in length. It had sharp teeth, ran on slender hind legs, and used its tail for balance. Terrestrisuchus lived 210 million years ago in Europe and measured 20 inches (50 cm) in length. It had a slender body; four long, thin legs; and a long tail. Protosuchus, 3.3 feet (1 m) long, appeared later in the Americas. These animals were followed by aquatic creatures, such as Metriorhynchus — which was 10 feet (3 m) long. These animals were the first crocodilians similar to those we know today.

TERRESTRISUCHUS

METRIORHYNCHUS

Primitive ancestors of today's crocodilians.

PROTOSUCHUS

GRACILISUCHUS

APPENDIX TO

SECRETS
OF THE
ANIMAL WORLD

CROCODILIANS
Survivors from the Dinosaur Age

CROCODILIAN SECRETS

▼ **"Dwarf" crocodilian.** Dwarf caimans measure a maximum length of only 5 feet (1.5 m).

Noisy crocodiles. Crocodilians produce many sounds to express messages. They can whistle, snore, and roar.

Heavy armored plating. The crocodilians equipped with the most armor-plating are Nile and marine crocodiles, which can weigh up to 2,200 pounds (1,000 kg).

▼ **A deadly weapon.** To catch large herbivores, the crocodile can spring from the water when its prey is drinking and use its tail to strike and stun its victim or break its leg.

▼ Crocodilian farms.

Special breeding farms have been established in different parts of the world to protect endangered crocodilian species from extinction.

1. What is the maximum speed at which a crocodilian can run?
   a) Less than .6 mile (1 km) an hour.
   b) 15.5 miles (25 km) an hour.
   c) 10.5 miles (17 km) an hour.

2. How many eggs does a crocodilian lay at any one time?
   a) Fewer than ten eggs.
   b) Up to eighty eggs.
   c) Over 150 eggs.

3. To produce males, alligator eggs must incubate at:
   a) 90°F to 93°F (32°C to 34°C).
   b) 97°F to 100°F (36°C to 38°C).
   c) 82°F to 86°F (28°C to 30°C).

4. How long does it take to incubate a crocodilian egg?
   a) About one month.
   b) About three months.
   c) About six months.

5. Which crocodilians are most dangerous to humans?
   a) Mugger crocodiles.
   b) Nile and marine crocodiles.
   c) Chinese alligators.

6. What is the name of the crocodile's oldest ancestor?
   a) Gracilisuchus.
   b) Geosaurus.
   c) Glypton.

The answers to CROCODILIAN SECRETS questions are on page 32.

GLOSSARY

adaptation: the way a living organism changes its behaviors and needs to survive in different or changing conditions.

aggressive: quick to start a fight or attack.

ancestors: previous generations; predecessors.

aquatic: of or relating to water; living or growing in water.

armor: a protective covering.

auditory: having to do with an animal's hearing.

carnivores: meat-eating animals.

cloaca: a common chamber into which the intestinal, urinary, and genital tracts open.

continents: the large landmasses of Earth, which include Africa, Antarctica, Asia, Australia, Europe, North America, and South America.

dehydration: the process in which water leaves or is removed from something.

devour: to eat greedily.

dominate: to take charge of or control.

duct: a tube through which a liquid or gas flows.

embryo: an animal in the very earliest stages of growth, in an egg or its mother's womb, after it has been conceived.

environment: the surroundings in which plants, animals, and other organisms live.

esophagus: the tube through which nourishment moves from the mouth to the stomach.

estuary: the lower part of a river, where the river's current meets the ocean tides.

evolve: to change shape or develop gradually over time.

extinct: no longer in existence.

friction: the rubbing of one object or surface against another.

gizzard: a muscular part of an animal's digestive system that is used for grinding food.

habitat: the natural home of a plant or animal.

herbivores: plant-eating animals.

incubate: to keep eggs warm until they hatch.

inhabit: to live in or on.

mandible: the lower jaw of a vertebrate.

marine: of or related to the sea.

marsh: a low wetland or swamp.

mate (v): to join together (animals) to produce young.

membrane: a thin, flexible layer of tissue in a plant or animal that lines or protects a certain part of its body.

meteorite: a meteor, or chunk of matter generated in outer space, that lands on Earth's surface before it has burned up in the atmosphere. Meteorites that crash leave huge craters in Earth's surface.

mobility: the ability to move around from one place to another.

ossified: something that has become bone or hardened into a hard, bonelike substance.

palate: the roof of the mouth, which is usually made up of two parts; a bony front part, called the hard palate, and a soft back part called the soft palate.

predator: an animal that kills other animals for food.

prehistoric: something that lived or happened before people began to keep written records.

prey: animals that are hunted, captured, and killed for food by other animals.

primitive: of or relating to an early and usually simple stage of development.

protrude: to stick out from a surface.

pulmonary respiration: breathing that is accomplished by way of lungs.

reptiles: a group of cold-blooded animals that crawl on the ground and have scaly skin.

salinity: amount or degree of saltiness.

snout: the protruding nose and jaws of an animal.

species: a group of animals or plants that are closely related and often very similar in behavior and appearance. Members of the same species can breed together.

swamps: an area of muddy land that is often filled with water.

temperate: moderate; not extreme; relating to climates with warm summers and cold winters that lie between the warm tropics and the cold polar regions.

terrestrial: of or relating to the earth, or land.

tropical: relating to the hot, humid regions of Earth near the equator. Tropical areas refer specifically to those regions that lie between the Tropic of Cancer (23.5 degrees north of the equator) and the Tropic of Capricorn (23.5 degrees south of the equator).

vertebral column: the spinal column, or backbone, which is made up of many small segments of cartilage or bone.

vertebrates: animals with a backbone and an internal skeleton.

ACTIVITIES

◆ Crocodiles and alligators are now endangered because they were legally hunted and killed for their hides. Do some research at your local library to find out what products were manufactured from their hides, and when it became illegal to sell items made from these hides. Also, as part of your research, compare the crocodile, alligator, gavial, and caiman populations in 1850, 1900, 1950, 1970, 1980, and today.

◆ From the library, check out a book on papier mâché sculpting, and model and paint your own fierce crocodile. Be sure to get all the details right!

◆ Find out more about the ecosystems in which crocodilians live. What other animals share their habitats? What animals do the crocodilians prey on?

MORE BOOKS TO READ

The Alligator and the Everglades. Dave Taylor (Crabtree)
Alligators: A Success Story. Patricia Lauber (H. Holt & Co.)
Alligators and Crocodiles. Michael Bright (Watts)
Amazing Crocodiles and Other Reptiles. Mary Ling (Knopf)
Endangered! Four-volume series. (Gareth Stevens)
Endangered Wetland Animals. Dave Taylor (Crabtree)
In Peril. Four-volume series. (Gareth Stevens)
The Moon and the Alligators. Jean C. George (HarperCollins)
Saving Our Wetlands and Their Wildlife. Karen Liptak (Watts)
Squish! A Wetland Walk. Nancy Luenn (Macmillan)
Swamps. Sheila Gore (Troll Associates)
Vanishing Habitats and Species. Jane Walke (Watts)
Wading into Wetlands. National Wildlife Federation Staff
   (National Wildlife Federation)

VIDEOS

Can Tropical Forests be Saved? (PBS Home Video)
Crocodiles: Here Be Dragons. National Geographic. (Vestron Video)
Cry of the Marsh. (Aims Video)
Reptiles and Amphibians. National Geographic. (Vestron Video)

PLACES TO VISIT

**Clearwater Aquarium
  Museum**
249 Windward Passage
Clearwater, FL 34630

Sydney Aquarium
Wheat Road
Pier 56
Darling Harbour
Sydney, Australia

**Armand Bayou Nature
  Center**
8500 Bay Area Boulevard
Houston, TX 77258

Vancouver Aquarium
In Stanley Park
Vancouver, British
  Columbia
V6B 3X8

The Aquarium
Marine Parade
Napier, New Zealand

The Montreal Aquarium
La Ronde
Île Ste-Hélène
Montreal, Quebec
H3C lA0

INDEX

Answers to
CROCODILIAN SECRETS
questions:
1. c
2. b
3. a
4. b
5. b
6. a